Subbing in the City

The A to Z of substitute teaching:
Recollections and recommendations for
substitute teachers, teachers, and
administrators in junior and senior high schools

Written by	Illustrated by
Sally Goddard	Arlene Armstrong

© Godarms Productions 2003

Note for Librarians: a cataloguing record for this book that includes Dewey Classification and US Library of Congress numbers is available from the National Library of Canada. The complete cataloguing record can be obtained from the National Library's online database at: www.nlc-bnc.ca/amicus/index-e.html

ISBN 1-4120-1524-3

TRAFFORD

This book was published on-demand in cooperation with Trafford Publishing. On-demand publishing is a unique process and service of making a book available for retail sale to the public taking advantage of on-demand manufacturing and Internet marketing. On-demand publishing includes promotions, retail sales, manufacturing, order fulfilment, accounting and collecting royalties on behalf of the author.

Suite 6E, 2333 Government St., Victoria, B.C. V8T 4P4, CANADA

Phone 250-383-6864   Toll-free 1-888-232-4444 (Canada & US)
Fax   250-383-6804   E-mail sales@trafford.com
Web site www.trafford.com   TRAFFORD PUBLISHING IS A DIVISION OF TRAFFORD
                                            HOLDINGS LTD.

Trafford Catalogue #03-1902   www.trafford.com/robots/03-1902.html

10   9   8   7   6   5   4   3   2   1

Acknowledgements

There are many people to thank for a project such as this. After listening to my moaning for a number of years, Tim, my husband, suggested that I keep a diary of what happened as I went to various schools. It was a great idea as I never would have remembered all that happened had I not kept a written record. Norm Armstrong advised, drove, and acted as a sounding board for many of our scattered ideas. Randy Hess helped with the computers and seemed to be able to get a printout when we thought all was lost. Linda Lentz guided our final copy. We would also like to thank Helen Mann and others who read the manuscript and offered constructive criticism.

To substitutes everywhere, this book is for you.

Introduction

There are several reasons why people become substitute teachers (subs or supply teachers) and many reasons why they leave. Initially, subs hope that they can find more permanent teaching through contacts in the schools. Once they start subbing, they find the flexibility in schedule, anonymity in schools, and minimal amount of preparation required are reasons to continue. Some stop subbing. Reasons for quitting include few opportunities for full-time teaching, a lack of respect afforded to subs from many students and some teachers, and a pay cheque which is dependent upon whether one is called to a job.

In most jurisdictions in Canada, substitutes are fully qualified teachers. I am qualified to teach Grades 7–12 Social Studies and English in several provinces. Most education boards try to match the regular classroom teacher with a sub who is qualified to teach that subject specialty.

I have lived in several different provinces in Canada. When moving to a new province, I have been required to requalify with that province's Department of Education for my teaching certificate. In some provinces, a newcomer starts off with a temporary or interim certificate, and after a specified number of days teaching, the certificate becomes permanent. One way to obtain the required number of days is to become a sub. My substitute teaching experience has been at the junior and senior high school levels as an English and Social Studies teacher. I have found that in cities across Canada, the issues a sub faces are all much the same.

The recollections that follow are based on real events that have occurred during the years I have been a sub in classrooms across Canada.

The purpose of this book is threefold. First, it is to describe some of the difficulties and frustrations many substitute teachers face on a daily basis. Second, brief examples describe the problems, frustrations, and, in some cases, humour as seen by a real substitute teacher. And third, in a section called, "In a Perfect World," suggestions outline ways that many of the difficulties could be alleviated, either by the classroom teacher, the school administration, or the school board staff.

Every year, school boards run short of substitute teachers. Sometimes it is because they have found alternative employment; often it is because they are fed up with the work. If some or all of the issues were addressed by those in a position to make changes in the way the system operates, then being a sub wouldn't be too bad. Perhaps more substitute teachers would remain as subs.

In the interests of protecting privacy, names of people and locations have been changed.

Sally Goddard

Preamble

For the fifth day in a row, the phone rang at 5:57 a.m. I struggled out of a deep sleep and felt for the phone. "Hello," I responded.

A computer-driven voice said, "This is the Automated Board of Education Substitute Employment System calling for Sally Goddard. Please enter your Personal Identification Number (PIN)."

I found my glasses, put them on, and entered my PIN number.

The system responded. "We have a job available. Press 1 to hear the absence information."

I pressed number one.

Again the computer voice came on. It stated the location of the school, the name of the absent classroom teacher, date and times required, subject area and grade level, and gave special instructions relating to the position.

The voice continued, "Press number one to accept the job. Press number five to hear the job again. Press number nine to decline the job."

It was a school I liked. I pressed number one.

Then the voice said, "We're sorry. The job is no longer available. Goodbye."

I hung up. It was 5:59 a.m. Between then and 7:00 a.m. the telephone rang intermittently for different jobs. Either the school was too far away or I had subbed for the particular teacher before and had found the lesson plans or the students wanting. Finally, just after 7:00 a.m., I struck gold–a full day at a school I liked in a subject area I was familiar with. I pushed button number one.

A

Announcements

As a substitute teacher, I often found myself in situations where I had no idea what the policy of the classroom teacher was relating to different issues. Announcements fell into that category. Each school handles announcements differently. At some schools, printed announcements are provided for the home room teacher to read to the class; at others, announcements are given out at the same time each day over the loud speaker.

In some schools, announcements are sacrosanct; no one talks, leaves, or moves while they are being made. In others, the students ignore what is being said and continue their chatter. On occasion, student voices may grow softer during the announcements but the conversations seldom stop.

Strange but True

I walked into an elementary/junior high school for an afternoon of subbing. I was escorted into the staff room by one of the central office staff and told to wait. I got the impression that the school might have had some problems getting the students to pay attention to announcements, based on the principal's introduction:

Principal: "Good afternoon students. I will give you 30 seconds to get to your seats and be quiet. I am telling you this because I have two very serious issues to talk to you about."

Approximately 2 minutes passed.

Principal: "The first issue concerns the car wash across the street. The manager came to see me this afternoon. Apparently, several students paid for a car wash but since they didn't have a car they used the hoses on their friends.

A number of passers-by were also sprayed. The manager is very upset about this. Can the students responsible please report to the office?"

Principal: "The second issue was reported by one of our school's neighbours. He often brings his daughter to the school playground to use the swings. He advised me that recently, he has had to bring a ladder with him to the playground. It seems that some people are wrapping the swing chains around the crossbar and he is unable to reach the swing seat. Can the students responsible for these actions please refrain from throwing the swing seats around the crossbar?"

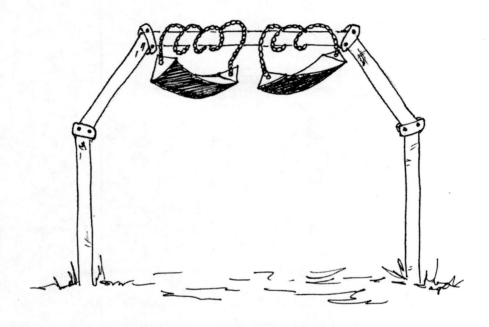

Principal: "No doubt you can understand the seriousness of these issues. This school has an excellent reputation with its neighbours. In future, do not use the car wash for student washes and please stop throwing the swings over the crossbar. Thank you."

Despite the serious way in which these announcements were made, the students were not running down to the office to report their guilt.

In a Perfect World
When a sub arrives at a school, the office staff should explain to the sub how announcements are to be dealt with. The sub should also discover what to do with students who refuse to follow school policies.

Attendance

In my experience as a sub, I have not found any junior or senior high schools with the same attendance tracking. Some schools use computer driven attendance sheets and the classroom teacher (or sub) must send the forms to the central office after the first period each morning and again, after lunch. Other schools require the teacher, or sub, to carry these sheets with them and check attendance in each class. The teacher, or sub, must remember to drop the attendance sheets off at the central office at the end of the day. There are some schools that have baskets for dropping off the attendance sheets and others have individuals in charge of attendance sheets and policies. Some attendance sheets must be completed in pencil so they can be machine read, while others are read manually so it doesn't matter whether a pen or pencil is used. Sometimes, upon the sub's arrival, the school secretary will give the attendance sheets to the sub, but often, the substitute teacher is not told anything about attendance policies.

There are other schools that do not have a computerized attendance system and rely upon cards. Each student has a card that is held by the homeroom teacher. If all the students are present in homeroom, the teacher sends a card to the office reading "All Present." If a student is absent, the teacher sends the student's individual card to the office showing a mark on the day of the month the student is not in attendance. Then the cards are returned to the classroom teacher's drawer or, in some cases, the teacher's mailbox.

The central office staff need an accurate attendance record. Throughout Canada, education is compulsory for all children of certain ages. Because of this, attendance records play a vital role in cases where truancy issues arise and proof of attendance or non-attendance is needed. In many schools, parents are called to confirm an absence. They are also notified when students miss a specific number of periods.

Those in charge of attendance issues need the information on the sheets or cards and work hard to get them.

Strange but True

Scenario #1 – The classroom telephone rings.

Sally Sub: "Hello."
Office voice: "You haven't sent the attendance forms down to the office. You are supposed to send them down before the end of the first period."
Sally Sub: "No one told me anything about the attendance."
Office voice: "It's in your substitute teacher package."
Sally Sub: "No one gave me a package."
Office voice: "I don't think the packages are ready yet. It's too early in the year. You must send the attendance forms to the office."
Sally Sub: "I'll send them down right away."
Office voice: "Yes, do that."

Scenario #2 (at a different school) – The classroom phone rings.

Sally Sub:	"Hello."
Office voice:	"You've sent the attendance down too early. There are students coming in late."
Sally Sub:	"The substitute teacher package indicated that I was to send the attendance to the office right after the second bell."
Office voice:	"That policy has changed."
Sally Sub:	"No one said anything about it to me."
Office voice:	"Well, I'm sending it back. Don't send it down until the end of the first period."
Sally Sub:	"Okay."

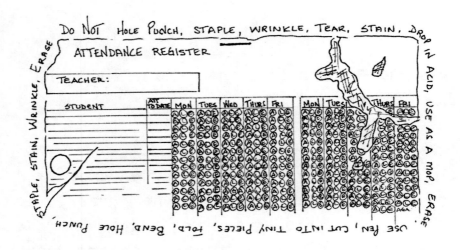

In a Perfect World

All junior and senior high schools in one system would use the same attendance documents. At the beginning of the year, as part of their professional development, substitute teachers should have the documents and procedures explained to them.

B

Beware

When the substitute teacher accepts a job that is described as Humanities, the person understands that it includes elements of English and Social Studies. More often than not, other subjects are included and the sub may end up teaching something that they know nothing about.

Strange but True

I was called to a school at the beginning of the school year to sub for a Humanities teacher who was going home due to illness. She stayed at the school until I arrived to tell me what to do with her students. There were notes on the board for the Social Studies and Language Arts classes but I then discovered that I was also to cover Band class. She described briefly what to do with the Band class.

| Classroom Teacher: | "The Grade 7's just got their Band instruments yesterday so let them make noise. They are really excited about their instruments. The Handbell option should be okay but make sure they wear gloves. The students know what to do." |

In reality, this is what transpired in that classroom:

The Grade Sevens arrived in the music room. I introduced myself and asked them to get their instruments out and see if they could make a noise with them. Out came the flutes, the French horns, the trombone, the tubas, trumpets, and clarinets.

One student found the paddles for the bass drum. There were about five students without instruments. Some excuses were: "I took my horn home yesterday to show my parents and forgot to bring it back," or "I wasn't here yesterday so I haven't got my instrument." These students drifted over to the piano and started pounding on it.

At this point one of the administrative staff wandered in to see if everything was alright. I said that it was but I felt that a period was too long for the students to just "make noise." The piano was particularly piercing. She looked at me and asked what the students were supposed to be doing. "Trying to make noise," I told her. She asked, "Can you stand it for the rest of the period if I take the piano players?" I readily agreed. Once the piano players left, the room seemed remarkably quiet.

The next period was Handbells for a group of Grade 7 – 9 students. Before the students arrived, I looked in the cupboards for handbells but couldn't find any. I asked the students when they arrived where the handbells were kept but no one knew. So I picked up the phone, and dialed zero (the office help number).

Office voice:	"Yes?"
Sally Sub:	"I'm the sub in the Music Room and the students are supposed to have handbells but there are no handbells here."
Office voice:	"The bells are supposed to be there."
Sally Sub:	"They aren't."
Office voice:	"Are you sure?"

Sally Sub:	"I am certain."
Office voice:	"Okay. I guess I'll find out where they are." (said grudgingly)
Sally Sub:	"Thank-you."

Luckily, the students were pleasant and understanding. After about ten minutes there was a knock at the door and in walked an adult carrying two suitcases. These contained the handbells.

The students got up to get the bells. "Make sure you put the gloves on before you touch the bells," I reminded them.

"Where are the gloves?" asked one of the students.

I dialed zero again.

Sally Sub:	"Thank you for getting the handbells but I am missing the gloves."
Office voice:	"Are you sure?"
Sally Sub:	"I'm sure."
Office voice:	"They should be with the bells."

I assured her they weren't.

"Okay," she said, "I'll see what I can find out."

After a few minutes there was another knock at the door and a student came in with a grocery store bag filled with white gloves. Again the students rose, put on the gloves, retrieved their bells, and sat back in their seats. I said, "Go ahead and play. Your teacher said you would know what to do."

"Where's the music?" asked one of the students.

"I have absolutely no idea," I replied.

I didn't have enough nerve to dial zero again, so I had the students return the bells to the suitcase, take off the gloves and return them to the grocery store bag. They then returned to their seats and it was decided that we would discuss any topic that came to mind. When the administrator came to the classroom this time, she asked why the students were talking and not playing handbells. I explained what had happened. She left me to it.

In a Perfect World

The classroom teacher should thoroughly describe to the substitute teacher (or the school board employment system) all of the subjects they are required to teach, not just the umbrella area to which they are linked. Subs should know if they may be expected to cover a food science class if the position requires a Humanities teacher. Likewise, an art sub should know if they would be required to cover a math class. This would allow substitute teachers the option of declining a job if they feel uncomfortable with the subject.

C

Computers

In the Humanities subject area, there are many projects that the students work on throughout the year. I have been in a number of schools where the students are expected to work on their projects while the regular teacher is absent. Most of the time, this works well, but I know there will be problems when the project is completely computer-driven.

Strange but True

The classroom teacher left me these instructions: "The students can complete their projects using the computers in the classroom. If there is room available, they can use the ones in the library and the computer room." There were ten computers in the classroom and 30 students. Only two of the classroom computers were working. I sent ten students to the library but they returned shortly. A nasty phone call followed from the librarian, explaining in very clear terms that teachers should always phone before sending students to the library because there were not enough workstations to go around. The computer room was no better. When I phoned I was told other classes had booked the computer room for the rest of the day. In addition, there were some students who had all their work on their home computers and so had nothing to do for the double period that they were with me. The 96 minute period was excruciatingly long.

In a Perfect World

Teachers should understand that if the computers are not working when they are in the room, chances are they are not going to be working when a sub is there. If teachers assign other areas such as the computer room or the library for the completion of assignments, they should make sure that these areas have been booked. It would also make the sub's work easier if there were plans in place for those students who have been working on assignments at home, and have nothing to do during class time.

D

Discipline

Experience has taught me that I go into a classroom with no real usable knowledge of that particular school's discipline policy. Can students wear hats in school? What is the policy on Walkmans? Do students need a hall pass to go to the washroom? Can students go to their lockers to retrieve books during a class period? Can the students eat in class? Can the students drink pop in class? What about water? If a student refuses to do anything or is causing a disturbance which interferes with the learning of others, what does the sub do?

At the end of the day, I have often found a list of policies pertaining to that school in the "Sub" folder. These folders are given to substitute teachers at the beginning of the day by the office. Sadly, I often haven't had time to read the material in the folder as I have been too busy trying to cope with the myriad of problems that appeared from the moment I opened the classroom door.

I have learned to call the office if there is something which needs to be dealt with. It is not a sign of weakness to seek help. However, the office has not always resolved the problem to my satisfaction.

Strange but True #1

A Grade 9 class was happy to find themselves with a sub for the afternoon. For some of them it was a time when they could visit; for others, it was a time to fool around. There was an extremely tall student, Bert, who had not brought anything to class so he had to go his locker to get a pencil. Then, he had to leave to get a drink, and then again to return to his locker for his textbook when he discovered it was needed. Another boy, Ernie, went to the washroom. While he was gone Bert found a bottle of Liquid Paper and drew a circle on the absent student's chair.

Of course, I didn't find out about this until Ernie returned to the classroom and went to sit down.

Ernie: "Miss, look what's on my chair!"

Sure enough, there was a circle of white paint on the seat of his chair.

Sally Sub: "Who did this?"

Bert explained that the Liquid Paper had spilt on the seat.

Sally Sub: "It's strange how the Liquid
                Paper made a circle. You know
                you have defaced school
                property. Go to the office. I'll
                phone and explain why I've sent
                you."

Bert collected his pencil and made his way extremely slowly across the classroom, laughing and joking with his friends as he went. I phoned the office and explained that I had sent this fellow down and the reason for it. The rest of the students got down to their work.

Within five minutes Bert was back with a cloth.

Bert: "I have to clean the seat."

The phone rang and the secretary informed me that the office felt that a suitable punishment would be for Bert to clean off the chair. When he had finished, I was to send him to the office with a note saying that the chair had been cleaned.

Now, to somebody sitting in an office this might sound like a suitable solution. The cloth he had been given was not wet nor did it come with any cleaning agent. It took him several trips to the janitor's office to get different cleaning agents. Nothing worked and he resorted to using a borrowed ballpoint pen to scrape off some of the Liquid Paper. The scenario was like a television show for the students.

Bert: "It's clean. Can I have a note?"

I looked at the chair. Smeared was probably the best description of the seat of the chair.

Sally Sub: "It's not clean."

Bert: "Well, I can't get any more off. Just give me the note."

So I wrote the note. "Bert has cleaned the seat of the chair to his own personal satisfaction."

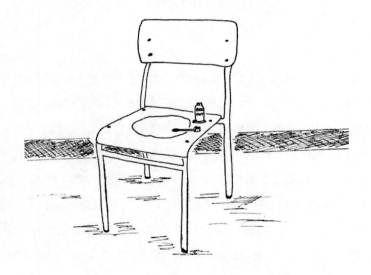

I was never asked nor did I hear anything further about the student's behaviour.

Strange but True #2

I had been covering Grade 9 Social Studies classes for a week while their regular teacher recuperated from surgery. I knew many of the students quite well having done a short term contract in the school and subbed there many other times. Prior to one of the classes arriving, the classroom phone rang. Another teacher asked if a mother could come in to talk about reading an exam for a learning disabled student. While she was talking to me, the bell rang and a Grade 9 class arrived. I said she could stay if she wanted to. It was a shortened period because of exams and the students were going to watch a video.

The woman's son, Arnold, came in and sat on the lap of a female student, bouncing up and down. He did not realize that his mother was in the classroom. When he looked around the room he suddenly saw his mother. His face turned almost scarlet and he quickly moved off the girl's lap . I didn't hear a word from him for the rest of the period.

Another student, Larry, said, "I don't see why we're watching this video. It sucks." An extremely heavy student, Mike, came in and threw himself at the desk before wedging himself in. "I don't want to watch that," he said in a surly voice.

In fact, the video had been started the day before and it fit with the syllabus. Except for Larry and Mike, the students had been enjoying the video. Once everyone was quiet, I started the video.

Larry began fooling around with the cords of the blinds, raising and lowering them. I went over and asked him to stop. He did but then said in a loud voice, "I wanta pee."

When Larry left and returned from the washroom, he made a point of blocking everyone's view by walking in front of the television. He threw himself in his desk. Then he found an empty potato chip bag which he proceeded to crackle. I went over and took the package from him. Fortunately, the bell rang at this point and the class dispersed.

The mother who watched the whole class, said, "I'd kill him."

I replied, "I am not here all the time. Imagine what it would be like to try and deal with him everyday."

I knew Larry caused a lot of grief at the school. The secretary confided to me that she felt uncomfortable having him in the office with her as she felt he was potentially dangerous.

In a Perfect World

Discipline is a huge issue for the classroom teacher; for the sub, it can be a nightmare. It would be very helpful if the subs were told at the beginning of the day how to handle unruly students.

E

Equipment

I can't count the number of times I have been left instructions for audio-visual equipment to be used and discovered that it has disappeared or doesn't work.

Strange but True

I was at a school covering a Grade 9 Humanities class. Everything appeared to be in order. The students were to watch a 30 minute video segment and then complete a worksheet based on what they had seen. This would have been an excellent lesson if the television in the room worked, but it did not. I went to the room across the hall to ask the teacher there for help.

Sally Sub: "Can you help me with the TV? It doesn't seem to work."

Teacher:	"Sorry, can't help you–perhaps you can try the storage room?"
Sally Sub:	"I see your TV is working."
Teacher:	"Yes, lucky, aren't I? You have to be quick around here to get the good TV's."

I hadn't been in the school before and had no idea where the storage room was or what to do with the students while I hunted down a working television. After several calls to various locations around the school, I tracked down a working TV which was available. But by that time the class was almost over.

In a Perfect World

Classroom teachers should ensure that everything to be used by the sub is in the classroom, and in working order. It's been my experience that televisions, VCRs, and overheads are switched or borrowed by other classroom teachers. I wonder if these teachers think that it's just a sub who wouldn't be able to tell the difference.

Expectations

A substitute teacher is a professional teacher who comes into schools to take an absent teacher's place. However, some schools expect the sub to do more than this.

Strange but True

I was at a high school subbing for an English teacher. I returned from the classroom to the English department room for my 'prep' period. Sometimes subs are asked to cover for teachers other than the absent teacher during the prep time, freeing the regular teacher for marking or lesson preparation. Nothing like that had been arranged and when I arrived, the Head of the department was there. I think she expected that I wanted to feel useful and cast her eyes around the room. They lit up when she saw a curriculum document. "Please go to the office and make six copies of this new curriculum. The office staff will show you what to do." I had to pick up the document with both hands. It was over 400 pages long, double-sided. It was not my place to question the validity of the job when, in all probability, additional copies could have been obtained from the internet or from the provincial department of education. So, off I went to the office. The office staff were wonderful, but confused as to why I was doing this photocopying. After breaking one machine, I got onto the school's backup machine. Each time the paper stuck, I had to get one of the office staff to open up the machine and get it out. After almost 50 minutes of photocopying only 100 pages back-to-back for one set, I returned to the English department room. "Oh, thanks," said the Head. "Perhaps you can sub for me when I'm away next week?" Perhaps not, I thought, but said aloud, "I'll check my book and let you know."

In a Perfect World

A sub expects to be busy from the time of arrival at a school. I do not expect to have a preparation period. I am happy to cover a class while I am on a 'prep' period so another teacher can mark or prepare. It is an expected part of the job. Even photocopying is fine as long as it is manageable and relevant. Like the students they work with, subs are quick to recognize busy work.

F

Fire Drill

An unexpected fire drill strikes fear into a sub's heart. If it is my first time in a school, I am not familiar with the school's procedures or the school layout. It is easy to lose a student during a fire drill. Luckily, I have found that the students are well-versed in procedures and I usually follow the flow, shut the classroom door, and hope that I have everyone. The students in the classroom are the responsibility of the teacher at all times and the substitute teacher when replacing the regular classroom teacher.

Strange but True

I was in a high school classroom when the fire alarm went off unexpectedly. At the time, two students were out of the classroom. One student was in a bathroom I didn't know the location of, and the other student was doing some photocopying elsewhere. The remaining students and I filed out of the school and waited with the rest of the school population on the opposite side of the road facing the school. I did not have a class list and had no idea who my students were, when mixed among the 2000 plus students at the school. I spoke to another teacher about my concern for the two missing students. "Oh, don't worry," she said. "Somebody probably pulled the fire alarm as a joke." This was no comfort as I watched two massive fire trucks arrive and several firemen in heavy clothing entered the school. I thought that the chances were pretty slim that the two missing students were still in the building, however, in the back of my mind, I continued to look at worst-case scenarios. When we were allowed back into the building (it had been a false alarm) the two missing students returned to the classroom. This experience aged me several years but, fortunately, the students were safe.

In a Perfect World

I watched a fire drill at another school during lunch hour. This policy might be adopted as way of accounting for missing students during a fire drill:

When the fire alarm sounds and the students leave the school, they line up outside by homeroom classes. The homeroom teacher counts the students present and then reports the number to the administrative staff centrally located to compare the numbers with the morning attendance figures. If there is any discrepancy between the two, an administrator could be sent to find the missing student(s). That way, substitute teachers would only be expected to count the students present, especially since they often will not know the students' names.

Food

Teenagers seem to come to school starving! I'm sure that their parents' feed them but it is sometimes hard to tell. The substitute teacher faces huge challenges with food in the classroom. Often, there is no school policy about it and the classroom policy is dependent upon the individual teacher. Students seem to snack continually, and then the wrappers and empty pop bottles and cans must be thrown into the garbage can, usually with an appropriate flourish by the offending student. This can result in applause or boos from the other students depending on the success of the shots.

Strange but True

Sally Sub:	"Please put away your chips."
Student:	"I'm hungry. The teacher says we can eat if we want to."
Sally Sub:	(to class) "What does your teacher say about food in the classroom?"
Class:	"We can eat if we want to. She lets us eat when we're hungry."

In a Perfect World

If each school had a policy about food consumption during class, and it was posted it in all classrooms, it would save a great deal of disruption for substitute teachers.

Fun

I have found that the best way to make the job fun is to look for and laugh at the unexplained and the unexpected.

Strange but True #1

I was talking to a group of Grade 9 students, mainly girls, one morning-the lesson the teacher had left was completed in about 20 minutes and there was still 30 minutes of class time remaining. I was working on a writing project at the time and wanted to find out how the students felt about body piercing. Several of the students had their tongues and eyebrows pierced. Suddenly, one of the girls said, "Turn out the lights. I want to show you something."

One of the students went over and switched off the lights. The girl pulled up her shirt and we could all see a glowing belly-button. The class took a collective sigh, as if in reverence over this. The lights came back on and everyone congratulated her.

Sally Sub: "How do your parents feel about belly-button piercing?"

Student A: "My mother just wanted to make sure it was done right so she took me to get it done."

There was mutual nodding in the classroom. It seemed that most students who had body piercing did it with the approval and support of their parents.

Sally Sub: "What about tattoos?"

One of the girls said that she would never have it done because it was permanent. Then another girl said that her mother was a tattoo artist.

Student B: "She has tattoos everywhere and every birthday she gives me one. We decide what it is going to be and where it is going to go. It's been like that since I was 12."

Strange but True #2

Most of the schools I have been in have telephones in the classroom. One class had discovered the telephone number of a person called Ed. When my back was turned, a student would sneak up to the front of the room where the telephone was located, dial Ed's number, and put the telephone on speaker mode.

"Hello, hello," responded the voice. There was a huge burst of laughter from the students. The first time this happened I didn't get to the front of the classroom in time to talk to the mystery voice before he hung up.

When this happened a second time, I did not know how to switch the speaker mode off, and this conversation was broadcast:

Ed:	"Hello, hello."
Sally Sub:	"Hello. Can I help you?"
Ed:	"You called me."
Sally Sub:	"I didn't. I don't know who you are."
Ed:	"I'm Ed. This is the second time I have received a call from your number in the last few minutes."

The students, at this point, were bursting with laughter delighted to have made two adults look like idiots.

Sally Sub:	"I'm sorry, Ed. The students in my class did this. I'll talk to

them but as I am just the sub it may not have much effect."

Ed: "Do that."

I turned and looked at the students. "Not nice," I said but, like the students, I could hardly contain myself. Luckily, just then, the bell rang for lunch break.

In a Perfect World
There should to be a place where these types of antics can be shared with the public. Often, people think that teaching is a dreary profession!

G

Good Days

There are some 'good days' as a substitute teacher. Often, these are single days that happen once in a blue moon but when I have one it makes up for many of the difficult days.

Strange but True

Here are a few examples of what constitutes a good day for me.

- I am given a number for a parking space and when I arrive it is empty and I can park there. When I double check at the office it is the right space.
- The parking space is close to the main doors.
- I sub for a teacher in my subject area.
- I actually get to 'teach' a lesson.

- I locate the staff washrooms and have a key that works.
- I can photocopy without needing a secret number.
- Another teacher drops in for a chat.
- Someone invites me to the staff room for lunch and actually sits beside me and talks to me.
- The kids are friendly and fun.
- The kids do what they are supposed to do.
- The office asks me what my day was like and actually waits for a response.
- My car is where I left it when I leave the school and is still intact.

In a Perfect World

These things should happen on a regular basis and be the norm rather than the exception.

H

Hand-in Work

Usually, but not always, I have found that students respond best to the substitute teacher if the work left by their regular classroom teacher is handed-in to the sub and then marked by their regular teacher.

Strange but True

The following list contains examples of assignments that teachers have left for me that really seem to motivate their students.

- Tests and worksheets that relate to what their students have been doing.
- Clear instructions with answers to questions the students might ask: For example: "Can I use my calculator?" or "I was away yesterday and didn't know about the test. Do I have to do it?"

- The classroom teacher has reviewed the test and has noted errors that need to be relayed to the students.
- Correct answers to worksheets that the students have been asked to complete by their regular teacher. This saves confusion over what is really the right answer.

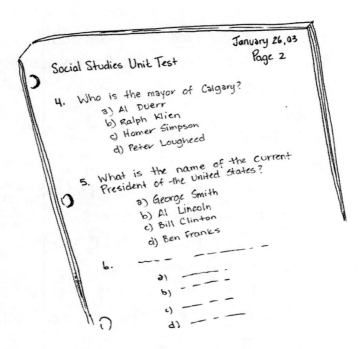

In a Perfect World
Teachers would leave assignments for the subs that they themselves would be happy to use.

I

If Only Their Parents Knew

For the most part, students view the substitute as just a necessary presence in the classroom. I have found that most students are polite and kind but at the end of the day, they do not remember much about the sub they had for Social Studies. It seems that substitute teachers are a visible presence in a school but at the same time, are invisible.

Strange but True

I was at a high school for an afternoon covering a Social Studies class. The teacher had left some notes for the students to copy and questions for them to complete. As students often do under similar circumstances, they began to talk to each other as they worked. I felt a little like a voyeur.

Student A:	"Do you have your driver's licence yet?'
Student B:	"Oh, yeah. I got it last summer."
Student A:	"Cool. I just got mine today! My Mom let me bring her car to school."
Student B:	"Watch out for the police. They'll stop you for anything. I got stopped last year."
Student A:	"What for?"
Student B:	"Drinking."
Student A:	"Had you been drinking?"
Student B:	"Na, not that time. But boy I was wasted a couple of days later. But there were no cops around then. "
Student A:	"What happened?"
Student B:	"Well, a group of us went camping. I was driving my Mom's car down this highway with my friend. I don't know why but we didn't have any clothes on."
Student A:	"When was this?"
Student B:	"In the morning. I think we were still pretty drunk. Anyway, the

front tire must have caught the edge of the highway. The next thing I know, the car rolled. We got out of the car real quick."

There was a pause in the conversation at this point as the three or four other students listening to the story actually comprehended what had happened.

Student A: "You mean you had no clothes on when the car rolled?"

Student B: "Yeah, and we thought the car was, like, going to blow up so we ran across the road and crouched in the ditch on the other side. Then nothing happened so we went back across the road, got our clothes and put them on. The neatest thing was that the car had landed right side up and was still running. So we got back in the car and drove it back onto the road."

Student A:	"Cool. What did your parents say?"
Student B:	"Nothin'. I never told them. The car was an old beater and they never noticed."
Student A:	"Way to go."

I really don't think the students minded that I was listening to the story. After all, I didn't count. I was just the sub.

In a Perfect World
Wouldn't more of these stories be wonderful?

J

Just a Sub

I can tell the attitude prevalent in a school toward substitute teachers by student comments made when I first walk into a classroom. If a student says something like this -"Great. It's just a sub; we don't have to do anything" – I can predict with reasonable certainty that chaos will likely ensue.

Strange but True

One memorable day, I was doing an afternoon placement in a portable classroom. The first students to arrive made the fateful observation, "Great. It's just a sub. We don't have to do anything." The teacher had left an assignment for the students to complete, but I was unable to get the attention of the class. I eventually wrote the assignment on the blackboard and indicated that I would be collecting the work at the end of the period. It didn't make any difference. The students refused to do anything and at the end of the period also refused to hand anything in. The next class was exactly the same. The students spent their time talking and playing cards.

It was difficult to know what to do. This wasn't just one belligerent student. It was the whole class. I debated, should I phone the office and say that the whole class is refusing to do any work? I decided that it wasn't worth the aggravation and left the students alone. I realized that this was a learned behaviour, and that whatever I did would not make the slightest bit of difference.

Fortunately, I was only at that school for the afternoon. There have been a number of calls to cover for that same teacher but I have refused to return. I would rather not work than have to deal with those types of classes.

In a Perfect World

It is the responsibility of the classroom teacher to ensure that students understand that the substitute teacher is to be treated respectfully and has the same authority as the classroom teacher.

K

Being a Keen Sub

As a "beginner" sub, one tries to do all of the right things. However, the initial enthusiasm may soon wear off.

Strange but True

Keen subs display their enthusiasm in a variety of ways:

- wear the board-approved substitute teacher label with pride;
- are totally obliging – willing to do anything for anyone;
- always arrive early;
- never have car problems or traffic difficulties;
- can read a map and find the school without trouble;

- carry a cell phone to contact the school in the event of an unexpected problem or delay;
- actually have the school's phone number in the car with them;
- go to the staff room whenever the opportunity arises and try to engage regular teachers in conversation;
- never call the office from the classroom to complain about a difficult student;
- have business cards available, advertising their substitute teaching subject areas.

In a Perfect World
The enthusiasm and joy for the job never disappears.

Keys

When I arrive at a school as a substitute teacher, I am always given keys by one of the office staff. I have to sign them out so the school knows who to contact if I forget to bring them back. However, most schools attach a large lead-like weight to their keys so my chances of disappearing with them are almost non-existent.

Strange but True

I don't think I have ever been told the purpose and use of individual keys. I imagine secretaries expect that through some form of divine intervention the substitute will find out. It's been my experience that often the keys issued don't work. Usually I find this out when I arrive at the classroom with 30 students waiting in the hall to enter. I have been in a situation where I tried each of six keys given and none of them would turn the lock. A student had to be dispatched to find another teacher from down the hall. Upon his arrival, he said, "Oh, those keys won't work on this classroom door. You need a different master."

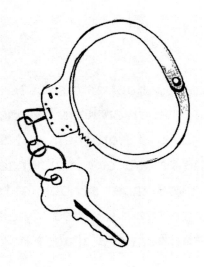

Sometimes, the school doesn't trust the substitute teachers at all and there are no keys issued. I've been told by one secretary, "Just ask the teacher next door and she'll let you in." Of course, when I needed to use the washroom, I had to find another teacher with the particular gender-specific key to let me into the right washroom.

In a Perfect World

Substitute teachers should be issued one key which opens the correct classroom and the staff washroom. Should that not be possible, it would be a good idea to assign a teacher buddy who can open all of the necessary doors.

L

Lesson Plans

All classroom teachers prepare lesson plans. This is a written account of what the teacher will have the students do daily. The newer a teacher is to the profession, the more detailed the lesson plans are. The older, more experienced classroom teachers rely on shorter notes as they have taught the lesson so many times, they know exactly what to do.

Lesson plans are the substitute teacher's guide for the day. When I see good lesson plans and a receptive class, I know I'll have a great day. Good lesson plans don't have to be lengthy-they can be very straightforward. For example, "Distribute the worksheets to the students to work on while they watch the video. Turn on the video. Collect the sheets at the end of the class." It is important that the students feel what they are doing is not just busy work and is part of the curriculum.

Strange but True

These are some of examples of lesson plans that have been left for me:

- Telephone message: "I just have to drive my wife to work but I should be home by the time you get to school. Call me at home and I'll tell you what to do."
- Creative arts class: "Let the students look at my wedding scrapbook and the scrapbook about my children. They really enjoyed doing that yesterday." (40 minute class)
- Team teaching: "Don't worry. The other teacher will tell you what to do."
- Telephone message: "You have the first period free. Call me at home and I'll tell you what to do."
- In lesson plan book: "Students are to continue to work on their projects." This was for a double period – almost two hours. Half of the students were finished their projects; some were working on their projects at home and had not brought the

material to school. Only about quarter of the class had anything to do.

In a Perfect World
Lesson plans should reflect what the teacher has been doing. They should also be available in print form upon the arrival of the substitute teacher at the school.

M

Messages

Although the computer driven sub line does its best, there are often gaps in its efficiency. I arrived at one school and found that classes were not going to start for another two hours as there was always a late morning start on that particular weekday. No one let me know.

Strange but True
These messages for teachers about the use of subs were found at one school on the main notice board.
- If your absence is on a Friday please take the time to change the start and end times for the day. It is very inconvenient for substitutes to arrive early for a late start.
- Please indicate your parking stall number when prompted by special instructions.

- If you have a prep the first class of the day, do not tell the substitute to come in later. We often need additional coverage in the morning.
- As you know, there is a shortage of substitute teachers. Please remember that Mr. Sub is available to substitute at our school. You do not access him through the computer system. You phone him directly and then let the school know that you have made arrangements with him to sub for you. (This must mean that this person only subs at this particular school and does not have to accept phone calls from Sub Placement starting at 6:00 a.m. I have not yet figured out how to do this.)

In a Perfect World

Correct messages would get to subs so that there would not be a lot of wasted time. Subs would not have to ask the office for a parking spot; that information would be provided. Subs would know how to get on a list for a particular school and not be phoned continually for others.

Make-work Projects

When a teacher leaves me a 100 question multiple-choice test at the start of a new term, I know that it is a 'make-work project' and that the real teaching will begin once the regular classroom teacher returns. Meanwhile, there are over 30 hostile students, angry at what they feel is a waste of time, tearing a strip off me, the messenger.

Strange but True

A teacher left me a 100 question multiple-choice test for a Grade 8 class. It happened to be the start of a new term and the students were excited to be back at school after a week away. The answers to the test were to be recorded on a scantron, a marking sheet that could only be read electronically if a graphite pencil was used. Only a few of the students had pencils. The policy at this school was in order to borrow a pencil, the student had to give the teacher something in return that the student would remember to pick up at the end of the period. I had sneakers, lipstick, money and watches littering the teacher's desk.

I handed out the scantrons, instructing the students to fill in their names, class and date before distributing the actual test. By the time I handed out the test, over 50% of the students had already finished. They had filled out the scantron without even looking at the questions and there was still 45 minutes left for them in the class. As the students were arranged in groups of four, it was impossible to keep those students who had finished from talking. It was the beginning of the term and the start of the day and there was no homework yet assigned. None of the students had a book with them. Four girls in one group had bubble gum and decided that they would blow bubbles and click their gum. When I asked them to stop, one of the girls in the group responded, "You can't make me. It's against my rights."

I walked away from the group. At the end of the class, I vowed never to set foot in that classroom again.

In a Perfect World
Make-work lessons make classroom control difficult for the sub. Lessons left by the classroom teacher should reflect what has been done or what will be covered.

N

Name Tags

One school board I have worked for distributes labels to Substitute Teachers identifying them as such. These are in a plastic sleeve and can be easily taken on and off and worn throughout the year.

Strange but True

I have never worn a name tag because I feel it calls attention to the fact that I am a stranger in the school. It also shows the students that I am not a 'real' teacher because I have to wear a label explaining who I am.

In a Perfect World

Picture ID would be better and more official. If all staff who work in schools wore them, a substitute would not feel so conspicuous in a strange setting.

No Information

As a sub, I am often not given the information that I need to replace a regular teacher in a school. I don't think subs need to know the challenging students. These become apparent after a few minutes anyway. I am concerned that often we do not have information that is vital to a particular student's well-being.

Strange but True

I was at a school, covering a resource classroom. The resource teacher traditionally takes students who need help with their educational program. I had been at the same school a few days previously for a regular classroom teacher. When I arrived I met a wheel-chair bound student who had been in my previous class. He offered to escort me to the resource classroom. Later, he appeared in the same classroom to have lunch. He and I were eating quietly together when suddenly he asked if he could borrow a Loonie from me. Normally, I would never lend students money but as he had been so kind and helpful during my time at the school and I had a

Loonie on me, I lent (gave) it to him. He went out, used the vending machine to buy some potato chips and returned. I then opened the chips for him. When his afternoon care-giver arrived, he was angry because the student was on a diet, trying to lose weight. "Chips," he told the student, "were not part of the Canadian food guide." The student was then taken out of my class and given a strict lecture for the next 40 minutes. This might have been a useful bit of information to provide to the sub before hand.

In a Perfect World

Subs should be given information that is vital to the well-being of the students in their classrooms. Teachers cannot rely on the students themselves to pass on the messages.

Out of Control

I have a feeling in some of the classes that I cover that it would not take very much for the behaviour to get out of control.

Strange but True

I was covering a junior high Humanities class at a 'good school'. There were two double periods for each Grade 9 class before lunch meaning that each class was in the classroom for almost two hours. The first assignment the teacher left was reasonably easy to supervise. The students could see a beginning and an end-not too difficult nor too easy. The problem came when, an hour into the class, many of the students had finished the assignment and handed in their work. The second assignment was a practice exam that was not going to be marked or collected. The students felt it was not important and would not work on it. So they started to fool around. Paint balls came out. Several students disappeared to the bathroom without permission. A couple started making paper airplanes.

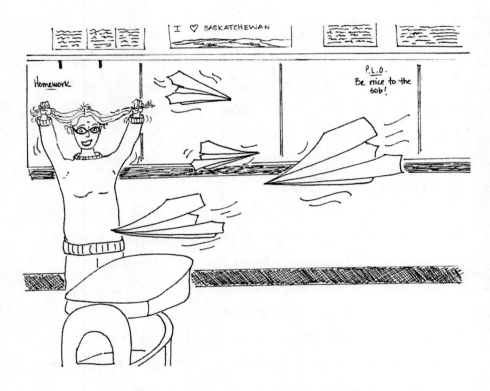

Some boys started to take other students' pens when they weren't looking, giving rise to arm wrestling and pushing and shoving by the pen owner to get it back. The girls got out their make-up. One girl got a pompom out of her backpack which caused enormous pleasure. These were not bad students but they were bored. If the class had gone on for another 15 minutes, it would have been difficult to keep control. By the time the second Grade 9 class arrived, I had quickly made arrangements for the students who finished their assignment to go to the library to read or do other work. With a change of scenery and a non-written component, the second class was just fine and there was no repeat of the behaviour.

In a Perfect World
It is important to provide students with meaningful variety, particularly during an extended class.

Outstanding Experiences

Like so many professions, there are negative and positive sides to the work. I have had positive and negative outstanding experiences as a sub.

Strange but True

I covered a class of 38 Grade 8 students for several weeks. Nineteen of the students were on Individual Program Plans (IPPs), which meant that they were unable to process information in the regular fashion due to learning or behavioural problems. The 19 IPP students needed additional help to understand and finish what was expected of the rest of the class. A few of the other students worked because they were so focused on their work that nothing could interrupt their learning. For most, however, the class was a chance to play cards or visit with their friends. It seemed that the minute I got one group of students back on task, another group would be doing something non-academic. I could understand why the teacher was out sick.

There have also been outstanding experiences of a positive kind. I arrived at a school for the first time. The secretary greeted me, and escorted me to the staff room. She remembered my name, and introduced me to two teachers. She said, "Why don't you get a cup of coffee while I find another teacher to escort you to your classroom?" The staff in the room engaged me in conversation. When my escort arrived, I was taken to the classroom, shown which keys to use and was told that if I had problems, this teacher was just next door. Because this kind of welcome has only happened once in my experience, I think it's worth writing down.

It's difficult to have outstanding experiences with the students since the substitute teacher spends most of the day trying to keep them on task. Occasionally, as a sub, you can tell a story or introduce a new game to the students which they might remember if you return to that school. But that's about as good as it gets!

In a Perfect World

If substitute teachers were assigned to only a few schools, then the staff and students would become familiar with them. Many of the difficulties experienced by the substitute teacher could be discussed and dealt with, rather than never being reported. Most subs know that little, if anything, is ever done about complaints.

P

Parking

Parking can be a nightmare, especially at senior high schools and at some junior high schools. Recently, I had the Chevrolet crest pried off my car in a parking lot of a supposedly good high school-somebody there must collect car crests. There is often no space close to the school for the sub to park. I arrived at one high school and was unable to find a parking stall. As a result, I ended up parking on a street about three blocks from the school.

I have since learned that if a parking stall number is not provided when accepting the job, to phone the school prior to leaving the house (if there is enough time). I will tell the secretary who I am subbing for and ask for that teacher's assigned parking stall number.

Strange but True

I was called to a school for an afternoon of subbing. The computer voice had advised me that the teacher's parking stall was #3. It was the beginning of the school year and I was running late as I was coming from a morning assignment at another school. There was a car parked in stall #3 but #4 was empty. I assumed that the computer voice had mistakenly given me the wrong number. I parked in stall #4.

When I went into the school to check in with the office, I mentioned where I had parked my car.

Office voice: "You'll have to move your car. #4 belongs to another teacher. She'll be really mad that you've taken her space. You should be in #3."

Sally Sub: "There's a car in #3. Where should I put my car? There's only 60 minute parking on the street."

Office voice: "Yes, there's a shortage of
                  parking here."

I went back outside, thinking I'd bite the bullet,
park on the street, and hope that I didn't get a
ticket. I didn't have much time as class was due
to start but the problem had sorted itself out.
The teacher who obviously used stall #4 on a
regular basis had arrived back and parked her
car as close as she could behind mine. I was
blocked in on all four sides. I would have to sort
that out at the end of the day.

On my return to the school, I went into the
office to explain what had happened. The
secretary said, "Oh, the teacher you are subbing
for hasn't left yet. That's why #3 still has a car
in it."

At the end of the day I found the teacher whose car belonged in stall #4, expecting anger. She was not angry at all once I explained what had happened and she moved her car.

In a Perfect World
- Subs would not accept jobs in schools where parking was not specified.
- Teachers should leave their parking spots prior to the sub's arrival or should make alternate parking arrangements.
- Schools would have specific parking stalls allocated for subs.

Photocopying

When I first started teaching there were no photocopiers in schools. Material which needed to be duplicated was typed on Gestetner sheets that used permanent black ink. Alternatively, material was written or typed on blue stencils that used a special alcohol concoction for the reproduction. These were not items that could be created five minutes before class. With the advent of school photocopiers, many teachers rely upon photocopied worksheets to keep their students busy when they are away.

Strange but True
The classroom teacher left a single worksheet to be photocopied multiple times for a Grade 10 class. The following conversation took place between myself and the school secretary, (who is often the guardian of the photocopier). It was minutes before the class was due to start.

Sally Sub:	"I have to photocopy this."
Secretary:	"You're a sub?"
Sally Sub:	"Yes."
Secretary:	"You need an access code to log in."
Sally Sub:	"Yes. I don't have one."
Secretary:	"You have to get it from your teacher."
Sally Sub :	"She's away. That's why I'm here."
Secretary:	"You need her access code."

Luckily, another teacher overheard this conversation, grabbed the sheet, asked me how many copies I wanted, and proceeded to photocopy using her own access code.

In a Perfect World

Teachers should try to photocopy material prior to an absence. In an extreme emergency, the school secretary should allow substitutes photocopying privileges.

Q

Stupid Questions

Teachers recognize that there is no such thing as a stupid question, however, there are times when people need to master the timing of their questions.

Strange but True

These are examples of awkward questions I have been asked:

- The school secretary of a junior high school, at the end of an extremely long day:
  "Have you had a nice day?"

  To which I replied:
  "I could have stood on my head naked in front of the Grade 8 class and they wouldn't have noticed. It would not have interrupted their card game."

- The classroom teacher I was covering for:
  "Can you leave your name and number and I'll call you again?"

  To which I would have liked to reply but did not:
  "Why? Your lesson plans are the pits. The students don't listen. No adult talked to me all day. I never did find the staff washroom. Thanks, but no thanks."

- A member of the administrative team:

  " Who are you in for?"

Sally Sub: " Mr. Write"

Admin: "Oh, I didn't know he was away. Is he sick?"

Sally Sub: "I don't know. The computer voice didn't tell me."

In a Perfect World
People should choose their words carefully when asking questions of a person new to their school.

R

Refusal of a Job

The computer has taken over the management of substitute teachers in many jurisdictions. As a sub, the computer voice system provides me with the first information about the job available-the school, the grade level, the subject area. After this, I have the option to accept or refuse the job. If I refuse, I must indicate from pre-selected sentences, why I am not accepting the job. This is the list of items provided:

1. Distance
2. Weather
3. Too short notice
4. No transportation
5. Illness
6. Inappropriate assignment
7. Previous assignment

Strange but True

At one point in my subbing career, I became discouraged with some schools and I found that I didn't want to sub for particular teachers. Call Display on the telephone allowed me to ignore certain calls. I think quite a few subs did the same thing. The substitute teacher board had hundreds of subs on call but very often did not have enough to meet its commitment to the schools. On one occasion, I was called by the substitute teacher placement office. To my surprise, the person knew exactly how many calls had gone unanswered, how many times I'd refused a job along with the reasons for refusal, and how many days I had worked over the previous months. It turned out, she indicated, that I should have booked off the system for the time I did not want to work, rather than refusing jobs or not answering calls.

In a Perfect World

Two new items should be added to the automated list of choices so that subs can honestly indicate why they are refusing a job. They are:

8. Previous negative experience at this school
9. Previous negative experience subbing for this particular teacher

If items #8 and #9 were collated regularly and then provided to the schools concerned, perhaps the substitute teacher board and the administration of that school could work with the classroom teacher and the substitute to resolve the difficulties. Such a follow-up system would place much more value on the job substitute teachers do in the schools, as well as allowing subs a voice in improving the system. As a result, subs would be less likely to refuse work when offered.

Rules for Students

Life for a sub would be so much easier if all schools had similar rules for the students to follow. Even if all of the teachers in one school enforced the same rules, and the rules of conduct were on display in each classroom, the sub's job would be less stressful. I recognize that this is not likely to happen but consistency would make the substitute teacher's job better.

Strange but True
These are variations of sample rules for students, taken from a number of schools.

Food Rules:
- Students cannot eat in the classroom. All food must be consumed elsewhere.
- Students may eat in the classroom. If there is garbage left on the floor or in the desks, this privilege will end.
- Students may eat in the classroom for the first five minutes of the class only.
- Students should treat the classroom as they would their rooms at home.

- Students may get pop from the machines at recess and bring it into the classroom.
- Students are not allowed to drink pop in the classroom. Water is permitted.

Washroom Rules:
- Students must have their agenda dated, time noted, and signed by a teacher. It must be carried with them to the washroom.
- Students leave the classroom quietly if the washroom is needed.
- Students must take the hall pass behind the door with them to the washroom.
- Students cannot go to the washroom in the period after lunch or after locker break.
- Students must sign their name and time of departure on the list on the wall before going to the washroom.

Telephone Rules:
- Students can use the classroom phone during locker break.
- Students cannot use the classroom phone.

- Students can answer the classroom phone when it rings.
- Students cannot answer the classroom phone when it rings.

Music Rules:
- Students can listen to music during silent reading as long as no one is disturbed.
- Students are not allowed to have CD players in the classroom.
- Students can use their CD player after all work is completed.
- Students cannot have CD players in school.
- Students can listen to their CD players as long as the music has no swear words.

In a Perfect World

Students tend to take advantage of a stranger in the classroom, especially one who is unfamiliar with the school rules. It would be wonderful if each system had a policy on rules of conduct for schools to follow. The rules of conduct could be included at the front of the substitute teacher's package to avoid any confusion either by the substitute teacher or the students. They would also be posted in each classroom.

S

Secretaries

Secretaries are the foundation of any school. I can often tell what kind of day I am going to have by the welcome I get from the school secretary. Frequently, I will not see another adult during the course of the day.

Strange but True

These conversations occurred in three different schools.

Scenario #1

Secretary:	"Yes?" (looking up from her computer screen).
Sally Sub:	"I'm subbing today for Ms. Wright."

Secretary: "Oh, not another one. I don't
                  think I have any more keys for
                  that room. You'll just have to
                  wait."

Another teacher overheard the discussion and
offered to escort me to the classroom. "Don't
worry," she said, "You're team teaching. You won't
need keys."

Scenario #2

Sally Sub: "Excuse me. I'm subbing today
                  for Ms. Wrong."
Secretary: "Okay. Here are the keys and
                  the sub folder."

These were passed to me by the secretary
who immediately went back to her computer.

Sally Sub: "Do I need attendance sheets?"
Secretary: "Yes."(as she started to work
                  again)
Sally Sub: "Where do I find them?"

Secretary:	"In the staff room, down there." (throwing her head toward a hallway)
Sally Sub:	"Can you tell me what room I'm to go to?"
Secretary:	"Room 300. Use the map in your folder."

Scenario #3

When I entered the office, the secretary came over to the counter to greet me.

Secretary:	"You have no idea how glad we are to see you. Here are the keys. Come with me to the staff room and I'll find a teacher to take you to the classroom. Would you like a cup of coffee?"
Sally Sub:	"Thank-you."
Secretary:	"Oh, and the staff washroom is just over there."

In a Perfect World

Subs should be made to feel welcomed and valued in a school. It only takes a few of minutes to greet a substitute as demonstrated in Scenario #3 but such a welcome would ensure the sub will return another time.

Staff Room

The staff room should be an oasis for the teacher. It should also be a welcoming place for substitute teachers. All too often, I find it feels like a private club where only those who are members can enter. As a sub, I have no idea of the rules of the club but I am expected to follow them. I am sometimes told where the staff room is, but normally, I have to find it myself.

Strange but True
I made my way down to the staff room after a particularly harrowing morning. I opened the door and was faced with two round tables with bag lunches on them saving spaces and some people already sitting in chairs eating their lunch. There were no empty chairs and I seemed to be invisible to those in the room. I tried to make eye contact with someone but was unsuccessful. There was an empty couch where I could sit by myself. I pretended to look in the mailbox of the teacher for whom I was subbing and then beat a

hasty retreat to eat lunch by myself in the classroom.

In a Perfect World

Teachers spend a lot of time making a new student feel welcome. It's a shame it doesn't often happen to a substitute teacher.

T

Classroom Telephones

As a sub, the classroom telephone is a lifeline to the office. It's wonderful if people also leave phone numbers close at hand so they can be readily available. But sometimes the classroom telephone is a source for meaningless conversation.

Strange but True

Scenario #1: Classroom phone rings.

Sally Sub:	"Hello?"
Voice:	"Oh, Mr. Teacher not there?"
Sally Sub:	"No."
Voice:	"Who are you?"
Sally Sub	"The sub."
Voice:	"Oh, okay. Goodbye."

Scenario #2 : Classroom phone rings.

Sally Sub :   "Hello."

Voice: "Oh, Mr. Teacher not there?"

Sally Sub :   "No."

Voice: "What's wrong with him?"

Sally Sub :   "I don't know. I'm just the sub."

Voice: "Do you know where he left his keys?"

Sally Sub :	"I don't know. I'm just the sub."
Voice:	"Do you know when he'll be back?"
Sally Sub :	"No, I don't. I'm just the sub."
Voice:	"Oh, okay. Goodbye."

School Telephones

I called a school's main number to confirm the starting time one Friday. Ten o'clock seemed very late and the day wasn't listed as a Friday late start in the School Hours handbook.

A machine clicked on after three rings.

Voice:	"Welcome to the district high school. Please enter the extension number of the person you wish to speak to. If you don't know the number, please wait and you will be connected to the staff directory."

Sally Sub: I waited ...

Voice: "Please enter the first three
                 letters of the surname of the
                 person you wish to speak to,
                 followed by the # sign."

Sally Sub: I hung up. I had no name.

In a Perfect World

Telephones would be used for what they were
intended – a lifeline between the classroom and
the outside world. It would be helpful if the main
line into the school could be answered by a real
person.

U

Unique Aspects of the Job

There are unique aspects to this job. The pay isn't bad considering the hours required. There's no preparation and, when I leave at the end of the day, I take nothing home except memories. I also learn a lot about schools and teaching.

I have also been witness to some unique experiences.

Strange but True

I was supervising a year-end exam and the students and I were told that the exam was to last for two hours. No one would be allowed to leave before that time. If a student needed anything outside of the classroom, the teacher was to call an administrator to accompany the student.

An hour into the exam, a hand went up.

Student A: "I have to go to the washroom."
Sally Sub: "You know I have to call an
                  administrator?"
Student A: "Yes."

So, I called the office and an administrator came
to escort the student to the washroom.
Half an hour later, another hand went up.

Student B: "I have to go to the bathroom."
Sally Sub :   "You know I have to call an
                  administrator?"
Student B: "Yes."

So, I called the office and an irate vice principal
arrived. She scolded the students:

Vice Principal: "This is the second time an
                  administrator has been called up
                  here. Not one other class has
                  called for an administrator.
                  Does this class just have weak
                  bladders?"

It was a redundant question. She wasn't looking for answers.

Vice Principal: "This better be the last time."

She escorted the student to the bathroom.

When the student returned to the class there was still half an hour left and the student had done all he was going to do on the exam. He proceeded to dig change out of his pocket, and using his pencil, coloured the nickel, dime, and quarter. After about 15 minutes, he had graphite all over his hands and his desk.

His hand went up again.

Student B: "I have to wash my hands."
Sally Sub: "I can't call the office again so you can wash your hands."
Student B: "Go on. It will be fun."

Needless to say, he waited.

In a Perfect World

Stories like this should be shared. It demonstrates what makes the job unique.

V

Value

Students are easily bored and they know when the assignment left by their absent teacher is worth their attention. Does it connect with work they have already done? Does it seem like the next logical step in the unit that is being learned? Does it relate to the students' lives? If the work has value, then most students will complete the assignment. If the students regard the work as busy work, not connected to previous work, and irrelevant to their lives, then they don't do it. They will use the period as a 'free' period.

Strange but true

I was in a senior high school English class-the fourth sub for the students in four days. They did no school work in the 1 $\frac{1}{2}$ hours I was with them. The students expressed the thought that the work had no value and was 'stupid.'

This is what happened. At 8:45 a.m., the first period of the day, I explained to the students what they were supposed to do. The following conversation was their response to the instructions.

Laura:	(eating three mini croissants) "I only woke up 30 minutes ago. You can't expect me to do anything. "
Jayne:	(drinking Tim Horton's coffee) "I've worked 40 hours this week."
Amanda:	(slurping a jug of chocolate milk) "You must get a big pay cheque?"
Jayne:	"Na. By the time I pay my car insurance and make my car payments, there's not much left."

Sally sub:	"Girls, you're supposed to be reading the poem and answering the questions."
Laura:	(brushing her hair) "I can't work yet."
Jayne:	(filing her nails) "I don't see why we have to do this. I'll never use it."
Amanda:	(now drinking coke) "Ya. Like, what's the point? I hate school."
Sally sub:	"So, how would you change it?"
Laura:	"Not come."
Jayne:	"Make it more useful. Like math- we just need adding and subtracting – none of that complicated stuff."
Amanda:	"And science – what do I need any of that stuff for?"

The conversation continued for the rest of the period and covered boyfriends, parents, clothes, and music. I was unable to convince the girls that there was value in what had been assigned.

In a Perfect World

Students would value knowledge for its own sake, not for what it would give them. A substitute teacher sees this attitude sporadically; the classroom teacher has to deal with it on a regular basis. It is hard to teach the intrinsic values of knowledge to students whose lives revolve around material objects.

W

Watch or be Wary

I always watch for the following:
- The location of the staff washrooms
- If anyone says, "Oh, you shouldn't have any trouble with this group."
- Preparation time
- Classroom power outlets
- Substitute Teachers' Appreciation Week (STAW)

Strange but True
- Few schools actually tell the substitute teacher where the staff washroom is. I don't know whether it is thought to be unimportant or just forgotten. I have been in the uncomfortable position of covering another class during my preparation period and then assigned to lunchroom supervision. There was not another teacher to be found

and there was no one in the office to cover my duties for a few minutes. I ultimately ended up using the student washroom.

- "Oh, you shouldn't have any trouble with this group" often spells disaster. It has been my experience that once the regular teacher goes, so does the behaviour.

- I now enjoy a preparation period, really enjoy it. I used to ask if there was anything I could do but then ended up with photocopying. I now go to the library and read and can be easily found if necessary. Once I ended up in a Grade 10 Science class. The teacher had been called away suddenly and had left absolutely nothing for the students to do.

- I check for wall sockets the minute I walk into a strange classroom. In older schools they are few and far between. If I have been instructed to use anything electric, power outlets are essential.

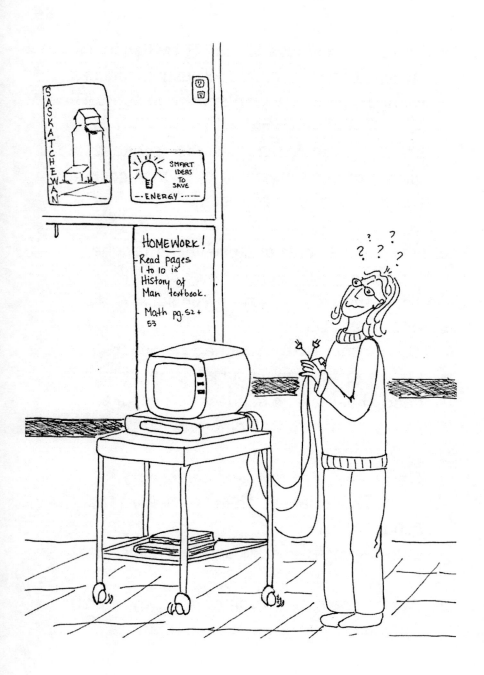

- In some provinces, **S**ubstitute **T**eachers' **A**wareness **W**eek (STAW) usually occurs without anyone paying attention to it. The last STAW happened when I was at a school where not one teacher spoke to me all day and strangers in the staff room were obviously not welcome.

The instructions from one provincial teachers' association gave ideas as to what schools could do to show their appreciation for substitute teachers. They included:
- Take a substitute teacher for lunch.
- Offer to take their supervision; they do need those extra minutes to prepare.
- Make a point to welcome and invite them into the staff room.
- Offer to share a lesson or activity.
- Introduce them to the routines of the school or the class.
- Leave complete plans and the name of a colleague buddy.
- Award them as Person of the Day: Guest Teacher.

- Provide substitutes with a mailbox, copies of the local, school and district newsletters.
- Organize an after school tea for substitute teachers at your school.
- Make up and present a school substitute teacher's kit: routines, policy emergency procedures, and so on.
- Most of all, remember, substitute teachers are professional colleagues. Treat them as such.

In a Perfect World

Wouldn't it be nice if the list given for Substitute Teachers' Appreciation Week would happen all the time.

X

X-Rated

As the weather gets warmer, students wear less and less clothing. It is often impossible to know what 'acceptable wear' is at different schools. One school may allow spaghetti straps with bra straps showing while another school draws the line at hats in the classroom. Students are quick to spot a substitute teacher and exit to the bathroom. They return transformed and wearing a completely different wardrobe.

Strange but True

Several girls arrived to a Grade 9 English class I was supervising wearing their gym T shirts. When they spied a sub in the room, en mass they asked to go to the washroom. I allowed them to go one at a time. As each reappeared, they had lost the T shirt and had on some of the tightest fitting clothes I had seen, apart from in the movies. It was like a fashion parade, and unwittingly, I was the master of ceremonies. Once the girls started, there was little I could do except watch the spectacle unfold. Obviously, they were not worried about their school-work – they spent their time concentrating on their appearance. There was little trouble with the class as they were busy waiting for the next girl to appear.

In a Perfect World

In each substitute teacher's package should be a statement about the school's clothing policy. In the event students don't comply, then the sub should be aware of follow-up procedures.

Y

You Want What Classroom?

At some schools, the original building is fairly easy to find your way around in. All the rooms on the first floor are numbered in the 100s, the second floor in the 200s, and the third floor in the 300s. I find it gets tricky if the school has had additions or levels in between the floors so I am never sure if they are at the 100, 200, or 300 level. Portable classrooms are often numbered 1, 2, 3 and 4 but the sub still has to navigate through the school to get to the outside door that leads to the right portable classroom. At many schools, the sub is given a map of the school showing the location of all the classrooms. What never ceases to amaze me is the fact that most of these maps are almost incomprehensible. Numbers bleed in together and if the school has had changes in the last few years, the map has not been changed. In this age of computer graphics and resource based learning, surely an accurate, legible map is possible.

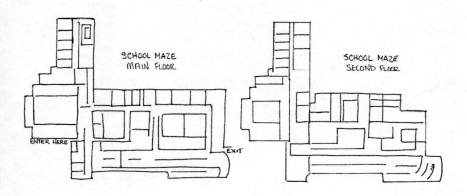

Strange but True

Staff and students will often try to help but they have their own code words for the route to classrooms. I had the following conversation with a group of students at a high school.

Sally Sub: "Can you please tell me how to get to the library?"

Student A: "Yeah. Go down there, do west up the north staircase ... does she go east when she gets there?"

Student B: "I dunno. I never go there. There's nothing much there except books."

Student A: "What about going the other way, past the pop machine and up those stairs?"

Student B: "Don't they go to a dead end?"

Student A: "I think maybe you should ask, like a teacher."

In a Perfect World
It would be helpful if someone could actually walk the sub to the classroom and on the way point out the staff washroom and the staff room. I like to go back to the schools that do this. I never return to schools where I am given a map, a key, and a shake of the head for directions.

Z

Some Days, It's a Zoo Out There

As a substitute teacher, I have come to realize that I have no control over things that happen-especially in junior high schools. What starts out as a normal day, can, by the end, leave me shaking my head. It's nothing I've done. Many junior high teachers believe that a full moon causes trouble. There could be trouble at home that a student brings to school, or the students could be outraged by a perceived slight committed by another student to a friend or by another teacher.

Strange but True

I was in a Grade 9 Social Studies classroom toward the end of the year. The students were to watch a video and answer the questions on a sheet provided. Two previous classes had done the work without incident. They'd handed it in when they'd finished and then used the rest of the period to chat quietly or do other work. The last Grade 9 class was also the last class on Friday. The students arrived, obviously not in the mood for work. I distributed the sheets and turned on the video.

Things proceeded as they had in the other class until about two minutes before the end of the class. I had my back turned and was collecting papers from one side of the room when chaos erupted on the other side.

A girl had turned on one of the boys and started hitting and scratching him. He just stood there with his arms covering his head. I could see that it was not a fight I could stop. I went out in the hall and called a student near the office.

Sally Sub: "Quick, get the principal or the vice principal to come here immediately."

He ran and I went back to the doorway. The bell rang for the end of classes but not a student left. The boy under attack had managed to move near the doorway. He shouted, "Help, I'm being raped!"

At that point one of the administrators arrived and the two students were escorted to the office. There was absolutely nothing I could have done to prevent that attack. Later it transpired that the boy had been bothering the girl all morning. In the class I was in, at the end of the period, he had gone to the sink at the back of the classroom, made a cup with his hands, and thrown water on the girl's back. She'd reacted.

In a Perfect World

In a strange classroom, many different incidents can occur. A sub has to be aware of when and where to seek help.

Conclusion

Subbing in the City has made subbing for me like a treasure hunt. Each foray into the classroom has provided me with new stories and strategies for dealing with schools and students. As I chronicled my experiences and organized them alphabetically, I have come to realize that substitute teaching is not for the faint-hearted.

Throughout the book, I have presented a problem, an example, and then a possible solution. None of the solutions involve schools spending any money. In order to effect change, teachers and administrators have to make substitute teachers feel that they belong to the teaching profession. It could be as simple as inviting the sub to have lunch in the staff room, or including a regular sub in a professional development day.

I continue to substitute teach. As a matter of fact, the phone rang this morning at 6:15 a.m. The job is on the other side of town in a school I have never been to. I wonder what the day will be like?

ISBN 141201524-3